It's Time to Celebrate

CHINESE NEW YEAR

Written by
Rebecca Phillips-Bartlett

KidHaven
PUBLISHING

Published in 2026 by
KidHaven Publishing, an Imprint of
Greenhaven Publishing, LLC
2544 Clinton St., Buffalo, NY 14224

Written by: Rebecca Phillips-Bartlett
Edited by: Noah Leatherland
Designed by: Ker Ker Lee

Cataloging-in-Publication Data
Names: Phillips-Bartlett, Rebecca.
Title: Chinese new year / Rebecca Phillips-Bartlett.
Description: Buffalo, NY : Kidhaven Publishing, 2026. | Series: Its time to celebrate | Includes index and glossary
Identifiers: ISBN 9781534549975 (pbk) | ISBN 9781534549982 (library bound) | ISBN 9781534549999 (ebook)
Subjects: LCSH: Chinese New Year—Juvenile Literature | Holidays—Juvenile Literature
Classification: LCC GT4905 P45 2026 | DDC 395.2614 --dc25

Manufactured in the United States of America

CPSIA compliance information: Batch #CSKH26
For further information contact Greenhaven Publishing LLC
at 1-844-317-7404.

Please visit our website,
www.greenhavenpublishing.com.
For a free color catalog of all our high-quality books, call toll free 1-844-317-7404
or fax 1-844-317-7405.

Find us on

Photo Credits – Images are courtesy of Shutterstock.com. With thanks to Getty Images, Thinkstock Photo, and iStockphoto.

Recurring images – Guppic the duck, spiharu.u. Cover – KanKhem, AnastasiiaM, Guppic the duck, spiharu.u. 2–3 – CravenA. 4–5 – Dragon Images, Savanevich Viktar. 6–7 – T-K-M, Tranle, AlexanderLS. 8–9 – PR Image Factory, Anirut Krisanakul. 10–11 – Fishman64, Svetlana Khutornaia. 12–13 – AlexanderLS. 14–15 – Prostock-studio, fizkes. 16–17 – FamVeld, Dragon Images, ChameleonsEye. 18–19 – Olya Detry. 20–21 – Sagase48, bayu pamungkas, wisely. 22–23 – Dragon Images, YIUCHEUNG.

Contents

Words that look like this can be found in the glossary on page 24.

It's Chinese New Year!

Hello there. My name is Min. Do you like my clothes? I am wearing my brand-new red clothes because I am getting ready to celebrate Chinese New Year. Chinese New Year celebrations last 15 days.

Chinese New Year takes place in January or February.

Chinese New Year can be on a different date each year because it is based on the position of the moon. Chinese New Year is also known as Lunar New Year.

The word "lunar" means "moon."

The Chinese New Year Story

The story of Chinese New Year is based on an ancient legend.

The legend says that long ago, there was a beast called Nian. Every year on New Year's Eve, Nian attacked the village. One year, a man arrived in the village and said he could scare the beast.

"Nian" means "year."

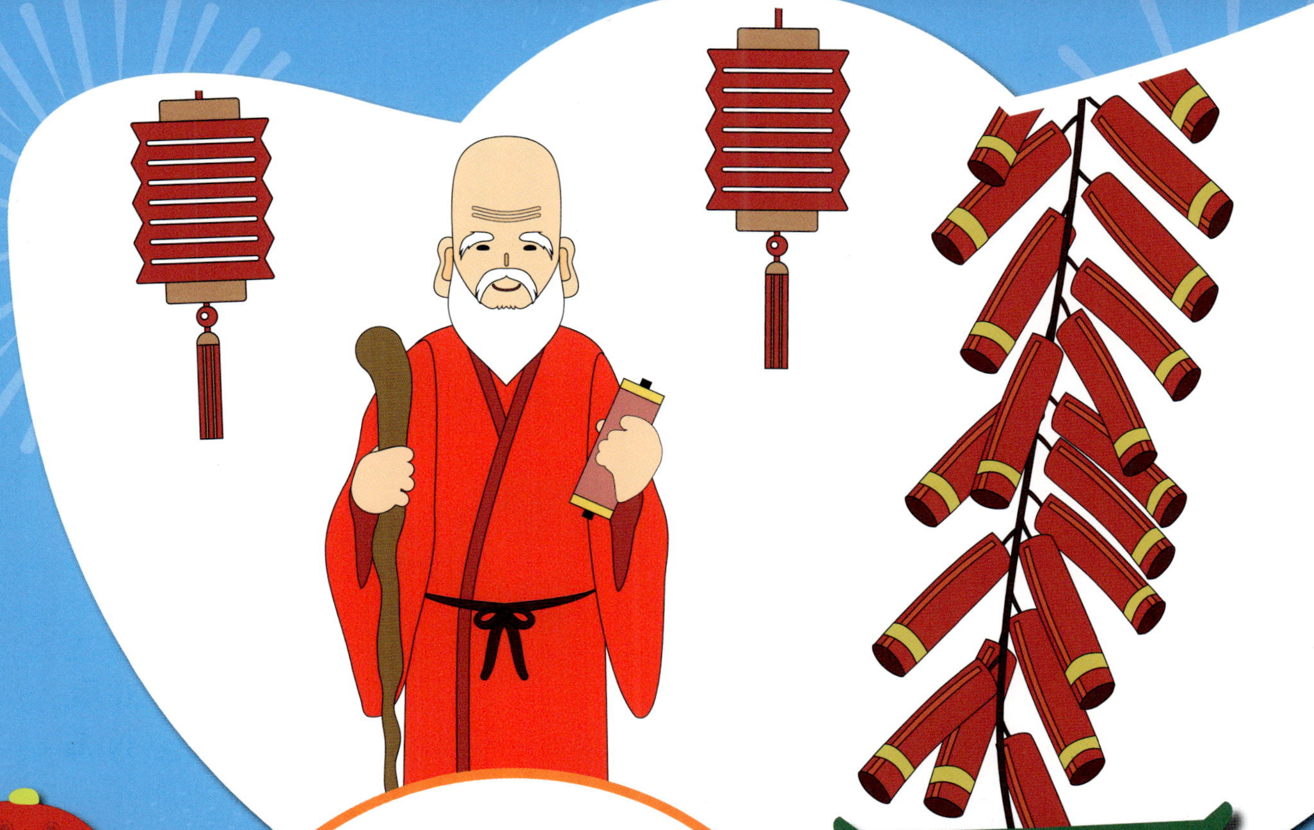

When the beast arrived, the man set off some firecrackers. BANG! Nian was terrified. The man then appeared wearing red and holding a lantern. The beast was so scared it ran away.

The villagers learned that Nian was scared of firecrackers, red, and bright lights.

Celebrating Chinese New Year

Many Chinese New Year celebrations come from the story of Nian.

A few days before Chinese New Year, we do some cleaning. Cleaning the house gets rid of all the dust. This gives us a fresh start to the new year.

For Chinese New Year, many people put up red decorations. Red is believed to be lucky.

Parades are a big part of the celebrations. Parades include puppets, dancing, and fireworks.

Can you spot how these celebrations link to the story of Nian?

Art Corner

Let's Make a Red Paper Lantern

Scissors are sharp. Make sure a grown-up is with you.

You will need:

- Red paper
- Scissors
- Glue

How to make a paper lantern:

1. Fold your red paper in half lengthwise.
2. From the folded edge, cut around eight lines. Do not cut all the way to the edge of the paper.

3. Unfold the paper.
4. Roll the paper into a tube. Glue the edges together.
5. Cut a strip of paper from another piece of paper. Glue the ends to the top of the tube to make a handle.

Meet the Zodiac Animals

Every lunar year is named after an animal. These animals are called the zodiac animals. This is their story:

Long ago, there was a powerful man called the Jade Emperor. On his birthday, the Jade Emperor called all the animals in the land.

The emperor challenged the animals to a swimming race across a river. The first 12 to cross would have a year named after them.

The first 12 animals were the rat, ox, tiger, rabbit, dragon, snake, horse, goat, monkey, rooster, dog, and finally the pig.

Creative Corner

Let's Write a Poem About the Animals

In the story of the zodiac animals, each animal has its own character. The rat was clever and sneaky and used this to win. The ox was strong and kind.

You will need:

- Paper
- A pen or pencil

How to write a poem about the animals:

1. Think about the animals in the story. What sort of characters do you think they are?
2. With a grown-up, research the zodiac animals to learn more about their characters.
3. Use your own ideas and the story to write a poem.

On Chinese New Year

On Chinese New Year morning, I put on new clothes. This gives me a clean and fresh start to the year.

My family gets together to eat a big feast. We eat our food using chopsticks.

Every year, I get a red envelope with money inside. We also give each other oranges.

In the evening, we go to a parade where there is a huge dragon puppet. The fireworks are my favorite part!

Craft Corner

Let's Make Firecrackers

You will need:

- Empty toilet paper rolls
- Red paper
- White paper
- Skewer
- Glue
- Scissors

How to make a firecracker:

1. Cut a piece of red paper that is big enough to cover the toilet paper roll.
2. Glue the red paper to the roll to cover it.

Scissors are sharp. Make sure a grown-up is with you.

3. Cut a circle, around 2.4 inches (6 cm) wide, out of white paper. Cut a line from the edge of the circle to the middle.
4. Roll the paper to make a cone, and glue it together.
5. Glue the cone to the tube.
6. Glue the skewer inside the tube.

Chinese New Year Around the World

Many people all over the world celebrate Lunar New Year. Each place has its own events and traditions.

In South Korea, Lunar New Year is a chance to remember family members from the past.

In Indonesia, religious people may visit the temple on Lunar New Year.

In Sydney, Australia, people celebrate Chinese New Year with a dragon boat race, even though dragon boat racing normally happens for a different festival in China.

It's Time to Celebrate Chinese New Year

Now you know the story behind Chinese New Year. You also have lots of ideas about how people celebrate all over the world. So, it is time to celebrate Chinese New Year!

How will you celebrate Chinese New Year?

Maybe you will decorate your house with lucky red decorations. Are there any foods or activities you want to try? Perhaps this year you could create some new traditions.

Glossary

ancient	belonging to the very distant past
character	what someone is like
festival	a time when people come together to celebrate a special event
legend	an old story
research	to find out more about something, often using the internet or books
temple	a place of worship
traditions	beliefs and actions passed down between people over time

Index